Last Word

poems by

Douglas Haynes

Finishing Line Press
Georgetown, Kentucky

Last Word

Copyright © 2017 by Douglas Haynes
ISBN 978-1-63534-354-0 First Edition
All rights reserved under International and Pan-American Copyright Conventions.
No part of this book may be reproduced in any manner whatsoever without written permission from the publisher, except in the case of brief quotations embodied in critical articles and reviews.

ACKNOWLEDGMENTS

Thanks to the editors of the following publications in which these poems first appeared, sometimes in slightly different versions:

Ars Medica: "Biopsy"
Bellevue Literary Review: "Alopecia"
Crab Orchard Review: "Elsewhere"
The Henniker Review: "Interlude"
Isotope: "Envoi"
ISLE: Interdisciplinary Studies in Literature and Environment: "Survey"
Terrain: "Corn Moon," "Bats," "Natural Medicine," "Last Word"

Publisher: Leah Maines

Editor: Christen Kincaid

Cover Art: Kent Ambler

Author Photo: Joel Heiman

Cover Design: Elizabeth Maines McCleavy

Printed in the USA on acid-free paper.
Order online: www.finishinglinepress.com
　　　　　also available on amazon.com

Author inquiries and mail orders:
Finishing Line Press
P. O. Box 1626
Georgetown, Kentucky 40324
U. S. A.

Table of Contents

Flight
Alopecia 1
Pick-Up Lines 2
Hunger 3
Spring Wind 4
Survey 5

Cages
Interlude 9
Corn Moon 10
The Man-Trap 11
Day of the Dead 12

Forest
Infusion Suite 15
Bats 16
Soliloquy in a Hospital Parking Lot 17
Natural Medicine 18
Biopsy 19
Elsewhere 20

Water
Endings 23
Last Word 24
Envoi 25

In memoriam
Tina Ray
1969-2007

Flight

Alopecia

Her hair was
a reason
I loved her.
It never changed.
She became
more forgetful.
Lines deepened
beside her mouth.
But her hair
never changed.
Like the softness
of fire, it returned
every stare.
It stood for faith
and what I couldn't
reach till I swept it
from the floor
like dust:
what the lump
in her left breast
made her,
what I feared
love would become.

Pickup Lines

She had shot three bears in her twenty-five years.
Her first one reared above her when she was twelve
pushing her sister in a stroller near their house in Maine.
She ran home to get her gun but forgot to bring the stroller.

As the party receded around us, I told her I've never seen
a wild one, but every summer in the woods I imagine
entering a clearing where a moon-faced sow devouring
berries looks up at me and says *I've been waiting for you
all these years.* The woman's lips unpursed and her chest
lifted slightly, as if to say that's everyone's dream.

She asked if I want to go denning sometime.
I pictured us pushing through a tangle of limbs
and leaves, pawing down a tunnel thick with musk.
The earth echoing heartbeats and heaving breaths.

Hunger

I place the head
between two nails.
With one hand, I hold
the scaly, yellow legs.
With the other, I lift
the ax. The pupil
fixes the falling steel.

The eye clouds, closes.
The red comb pales.
The wings pump blood
out the riven neck.

After plucking, the carcass
hangs from the rafters:
a pink satellite like my hand
once slick with heart and lungs
flying across a woman's thigh.

Spring Wind

Nimbus clouds march like tortoises
teased by swards they can never reach.

I forget a thousand small kisses
aspiring for the perfect one.

Is happiness just an absence
of dissatisfaction?

Or is the jolt of pleasure when I wake
to the soft sea behind her ears

proof that joy strikes over and over
like grass greening every April

in the time it takes to eat a bowl of oatmeal?
Once, I suspected all the knives in the room

of plotting crimes against humanity.
I saw no difference between dormant

and dead. She wasn't there
to teach me trees tremble with electrons.

Now the weather isn't
what could happen but what has:

branches swaying like the arms I feel
before she even opens them.

We say wind comes from a direction,
but where does it begin?

Survey

*Last year my husband counted with me
and could see each bird from here*
the widow kept saying while she and I tallied
the golden plovers blackening the bay's far shore.

I guessed there were five thousand.
More than that, and he's one of them she said.
The wind that swept us all morning slackened,
and the plovers stretched their angled wings.

As they lifted, the sun broke the clouds.
The flock split so the light flared between
the two groups of birds like an invitation
for good souls to enter heaven's open door.

Simile is even more simple-minded than memory,
but I couldn't say that when her only solace
was this one bird that left the two flocks
and flew straight toward the sun.

Cages

Interlude

It's over in seconds
the blue-backed swallow
furiously winging
to kiss cloaca against
cloaca just long enough
for this to happen again
on these power lines
bringing light
to a woman's eyes
that leads a man
to say he loves her
hoping this time
the coop of language
will hold feeling fast
though he knows
words are like swallows
blown from their mates
by the wind

Corn Moon

Husband and wife are just two people who can look away from each other
like strangers passing in the street. Summer's aspirations have strewn

the sidewalks with acorns. No one ever asks if you had a good winter.
Bikinis become sweaters at sundown. Crickets scissor the night.

Every time I speak to her she cries. The barred moonrise is like
arriving in a new country knowing you'll stay just long enough

to miss what you've left when you leave. The last morning glories bloom
and wither like unnamed stars. Why do I want to capture the word

for their color: not violet, not blue? In ten thousand years of domesticity
we've invented nothing but cages to keep creatures we need from leaving.

The Man-Trap

> "Were the inventors of automatic machines to be ranged according to the excellence of their devices for producing sound artistic torture, the creator of the man-trap would occupy a very respectable, if not a very high place."
> —*Thomas Hardy, The Woodlanders*

When the hunchbacked man cleaning the toilets at work
says *Hello, my mother told me to shave, comb my hair,
dress nice because that's what people do to be accepted*
I reconsider my reluctance to go home, where my wife
said goodbye this morning with a crystalline smile
just asking to be shattered, the only gesture she knew
would allow her to leave without having to kiss me.

The man tells me his name—a name we share—
which pleases him, and we wish each other good night,
a wish I mean, maybe the first sincere words I've said
all day as I've wondered if marriage leads to anything
but misplaced torture, a perfect design for mutual infliction
of character flaws like Hardy's iron circle of spikes
that halves itself on his heroine's taffeta dress
instead of on her philandering husband.

Back home I sit through another speechless dinner—
almost resigned to a love that risks no loss of composure—
till my encounter with the janitor strikes as quick
as that trap. I tell my wife how happy he was
just to talk and have a job, and I weep
when she takes me in her arms.

Day of the Dead

A month-old baby's grave covered with pine needles
and birds of paradise in green soda bottles.

A woman twisting black stilettos
in a sore of red earth.

Children flying kites made of plastic bags
and popsicle sticks.

Men sitting on tombstones selling gum
and single cigarettes.

A wooden casket floating
on the murmurous hymns of mourners

mixed with distant marimba strains
of "Guantanamera."

A man splashing marigold petals
in the shape of a cross on a grave

who turns to me and says
You must be here to see the living.

Forest

Infusion Suite

You have to live every moment to the fullest the middle-aged man says
while a plastic port in his arm passes poison into a pierced vein.

Once a month, he'll sit here all day till the tumors or the poison
take him. He nods off in his leather recliner. There's nothing else to do

but watch soap operas, listen to the bald children chattering
in their corner, and let the clear elixir fall through the forest of tubes

drop by measured drop, so much like the slow end of summer rain
that numb fingers and barren wombs and stomachs turning inside out

seem like afflictions that can only strike someone else.

Bats

The body remembers
like summer dusk
in a northern country
where evening's broken skin
blurs the horizon
for what seems another day
as if the separate incarnations
of time and matter
were collapsing
and my shudder
at the bats' rush
from beneath the roof
like the sound of rain
became my knees buckling
as they wheeled her
into surgery
and the wings diving
from the eaves
became the scalpel
bent toward her breast
that didn't veer away

Soliloquy in a Hospital Parking Lot

My undone, imagined child, how can I tell you not to fear the dark
when I dread it myself? How can I father the idea you'll always be?

I could say medicine's the art of making the body inhospitable,
but solace means nothing to you. You don't even want to be born.

You can't be mourned any more than the plastic legs
of the man hobbling toward me can replace the grief of flesh

or his fake arms can feel the wind. It's cruel to pit limbs against lives
as if loss could be settled by a score. But counting pain soothes me:

I'm not your never-to-be mother irradiated, carved, and chemoed;
not the quadriplegic who smiles when I say good morning

with guilty satisfaction; not you in the darkness that holds
no horror because you don't know it's everlasting.

Natural Medicine

The doctor tells her to lift her johnny way up over her head,
puts a cold stethoscope on her back, and says *Breathe deeply*.

I stop breathing. I imagine her lungs burbling like boiling water.
The doctor says *Let's take a look*. She and I don't look.

Looks good which means that though one breast is a rift
of scars the other seems fine. *But you're not out of the woods yet*

which means death lurks like a toothy beast behind every tree,
but the forest ends just beyond the horizon, means that the doctor

doesn't want to say that no medicine from a rainforest fern
or social-climbing bacterium can rubber-stamp her saved.

He says *Here's what we'll do* because he gets paid to do something
despite knowing the body's mysteries haven't faded as fast

as the rainforest or the family farm, as the path outward
with no moon to light the way, where if she lies down to sleep

nature won't wake her in the morning.

Biopsy

When the doctor found a thin cord
where her left breast was,
the ground rushed toward me.
But we're not to worry.
It could be a nerve enflamed
from losing the flesh around it.
It could be another tumor.

We wait watching young phoebes
fall from their nest in the eaves:
the shove and flutter that spells
the future of flight each time
as if wings had to be reinvented
for all new birds to thwart
gravity's thud, as if uncertainty
had nothing to do with death.

Mornings open with inventories
of skin and dreams receding like days
our bodies never lived.
Whether or not we worry,
our bones stretch each hour's chance
like the fledglings' hollow wings.

Elsewhere

A handful of days every year
the birches become the color
of what I have
and what I don't,

untouchable as steam
lifting from a woman's shoulders
in the shower while snow gathers
on the apple green leaves.

I'm tired of looking at the earth
for images of the body
and at the body
for images of the earth.

The no man's land of metaphor
leaves me mute,
unable to be anywhere
without imagining another place.

I want my gaze to take me
where words part from things.
To devote your life to art
or anyone is to live in two worlds,

to move back and forth
through the distance between
beloved and your hands.
Wanting won't get you any closer.

Water

Endings

Once, on my knees beside her bed, I said I could give her everything
she wanted if she just gave me time. She stared out the window
at white horses. We became like a bed of leftover coals

too cold to start a fire in the morning. The land refused
to console like the heroine's last words in a tragic romance:
I have loved. I will love. My only comfort when I left for good

was the highway's hum of strangers summoned by the warm familiar
like my longing to stay one more night lost in the coil of the past.
Driving away beneath a beet-red moon, I remembered holding her

by the River Shannon with my last unwillingness to let go.
I wanted a foreign country to make us kinder,
more aware of the desires our gestures betrayed:

my fingers reaching for her vanished curls,
her hands splayed across my chest as if to push off any moment
like the nearby boats moored with fraying ropes.

When two irreconcilable lives release each other from the grasp of habit
and lay down groping darkness miles apart, they drift like expended stars
through nights no memory nor idea of marriage can end.

Last Word

She ate a piece of tuna and a piece of salmon, raw on my fingers
passing her blue, faintly upturned lips. The chef spent half an hour
of her final day arraying the fish in tiny bites and festooning them
with saw-toothed plastic. I ate what she couldn't the day after she died,

when her last everythings became decoration: the book
she wanted on her bed but never finished; her smile in the picture
donning her pink wig; the red straw she sipped coffee through before
slipping unconscious. When the rasp and moan of her death rattle hushed,

I was reading about ceviche in a magazine I'd bought too late
for her to read. I reached her just in time to see her eyes roll
and dilate, to hear her shallow penultimate breaths
more like preparation for stillness than actual gasps of air.

The wood frog chorus outside went on. If someone you love is dying,
decide whether you believe in ghosts. Without the map of belief,
train whistles in the night that I used to hear beside her
became bearers of someone I couldn't touch.

Wind thrumming a window screen sounded like a whisper.
Do you say hello to the dead? Or just start with what you wish
you had said, since the space between words and a world without them
won't survive your sleepless night in the room beside her body?

The next morning arrived like houselights after a tragedy's curtain falls,
like the crowd's transformation that isn't fulfillment in the face
of someone else's misfortune, but gratitude that the heroine believed
stubbornly in redemption. Her last word was *water*.

Envoi

Not since hay was down and harriers
coursed the sweet-smelling fields,
not since she came home from the doctor
saying cancer, have I pulled off the road
just to look at birds. Not since landscape
lost its symbols. Now the lakes
are freezing over. In the river,
gulls and mergansers gather.
I get out of the car. They flush downstream
trailing white edges of wings on the rapids:
tilted flashes of light that can't last.
The car is running. Log trucks roar by.
Trees are money in this mill town, and snow
softens nothing. If anyone sees me here,
tell them I'm all right. Tell them no body
of water can touch me, and if I'm wrong
I felt joy at the very last second.

Douglas Haynes grew up in Iowa and Illinois and earned an MFA in creative writing from Southern Illinois University Carbondale. He also studied languages and literature in Germany, Ireland, Guatemala, and Mexico. After years of world wandering, he returned to the Upper Midwest, where he is an associate professor of English at the University of Wisconsin Oshkosh.

Haynes's poems and translations of German and Irish poetry have appeared in *Bellevue Literary Review, Crab Orchard Review, Poetry Ireland Review, Terrain* and many other journals in the US, Canada, and Europe. *Last Word* is his first collection of poetry. His essays and journalism are also widely published, and he is the author of the narrative nonfiction book *Every Day We Live Is the Future: Surviving in a City of Disasters* (University of Texas Press).

He lives with his family in Madison, Wisconsin between a lake, a corn field, and an abandoned feed mill. More about him and his work can be found on his website: www.douglas-haynes.com.

www.ingramcontent.com/pod-product-compliance
Lightning Source LLC
LaVergne TN
LVHW051614080426
835510LV00020B/3282